CONTENTS

IS A SHETLAND SHEEPDOG RIGHT FOR YOU?

The sweet Shetland sheepdog makes a great family pet. It is a very active dog. If your family is active, the Shetland sheepdog might be right for you.

The Shetland sheepdog is also known as a Sheltie.

A DOG OR A PUPPY?

Shetland sheepdogs are quick and ready to learn. But training any dog takes time. If you do not have time to train a puppy, you may want an older Shetland sheepdog instead.

Shetland sheepdogs come from the Shetland Islands of Scotland.

LOVING YOUR SHETLAND SHEEPDOG

Love your Shetland sheepdog by teaching her new tricks! Reward her with a special treat. She will also love to play and cuddle with you!

Shetland sheepdogs do well in obedience and agility contests.

EXERCISE

Shetland sheepdogs need long walks or hikes on a leash. A game of fetch will help keep your dog busy.

FEEDING YOUR SHETLAND SHEEPDOG

Shetland sheepdogs can be fed wet or dry dog food. Ask a veterinarian (vet), a doctor for animals, which food is best for your dog and how much to feed her.

Give your Shetland sheepdog fresh, clean water every day.

Remember to keep your dog's food and water dishes clean. Dirty dishes can make a dog sick.

Do not feed your dog people food. It can make her sick.

Your new dog will need:

a collar with a tag

a bed

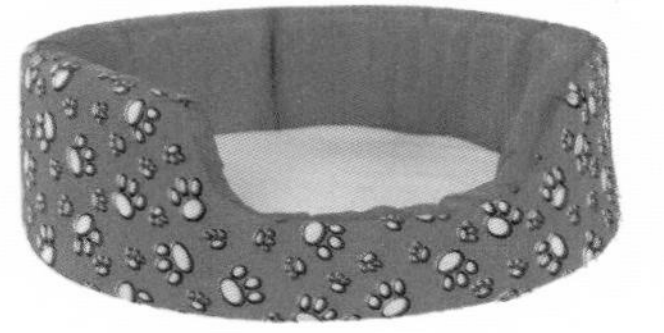

a brush

food and water dishes

a leash

toys

Shetland sheepdogs are clean dogs. They will lick and groom themselves every day.

GROOMING

Shetland sheepdogs shed a lot. This means their hair falls out. They should be brushed often and bathed only when needed. Make sure you use shampoo made specially for dogs.

Your Shetland sheepdog's nails will need to be clipped. A vet or groomer can show you how. Your dog's ears should be cleaned, and his teeth should be brushed by an adult.

WHAT YOU SHOULD KNOW

Shetland sheepdogs bark more than most dogs. They make good watchdogs.

They like to chase moving things such as cars. Keep your dog fenced in or on a leash when outside.

Shetland sheepdogs are peaceful dogs that do best in a quiet home.

Shetland sheepdogs are so smart,
they can be trained to
help sick people.

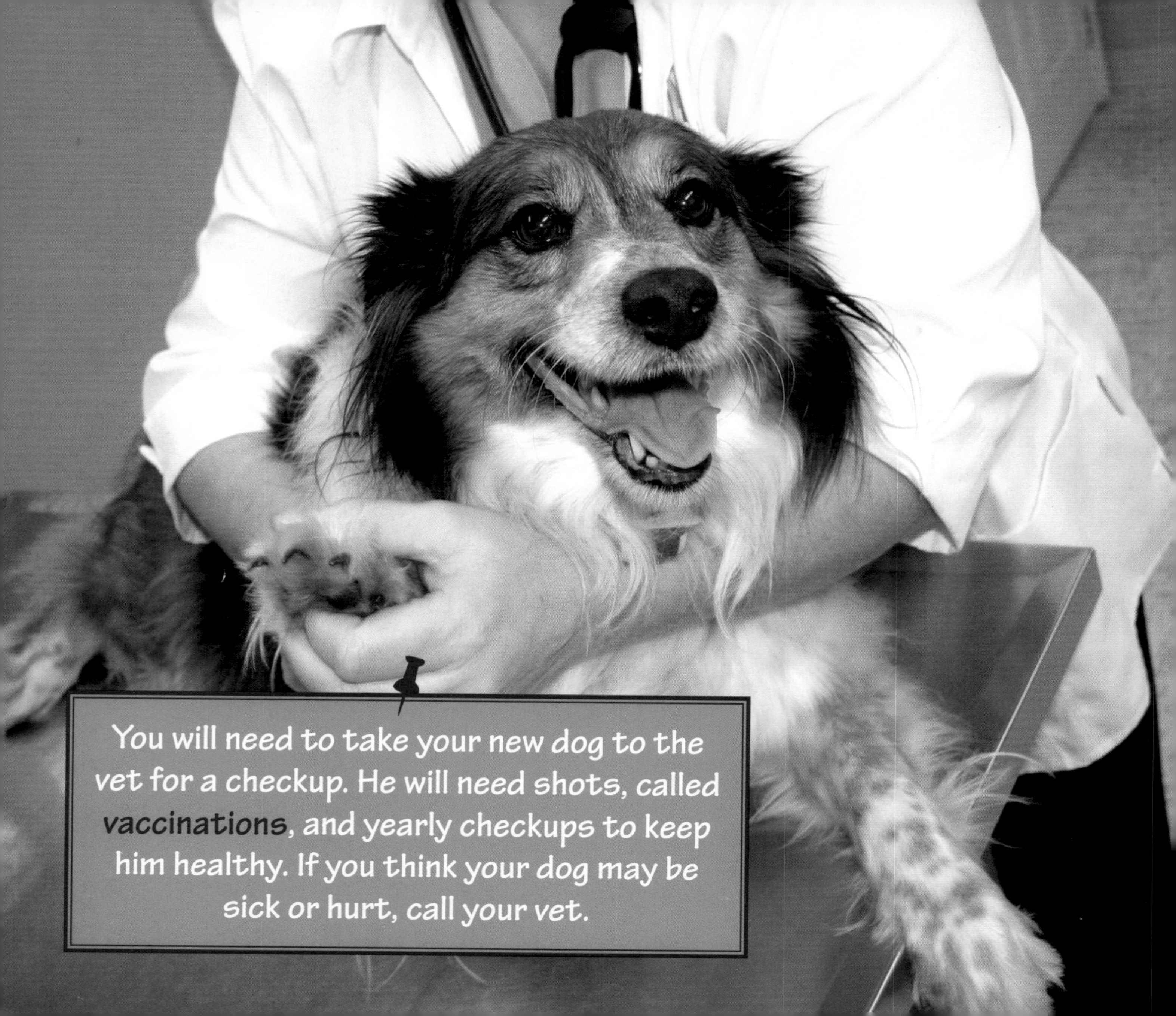

You will need to take your new dog to the vet for a checkup. He will need shots, called **vaccinations**, and yearly checkups to keep him healthy. If you think your dog may be sick or hurt, call your vet.

A GOOD FRIEND

When not doing tricks, your Shetland sheepdog will enjoy spending time with you. She may follow you around everywhere you go!

A healthy Shetland sheepdog can live as long as 15 years.

NOTE TO PARENTS

It is important to consider having your dog spayed or neutered when the dog is young. Spaying and neutering are operations that prevent unwanted puppies and can help improve the overall health of your dog.

It is also a good idea to microchip your dog, in case he or she gets lost. A vet will implant a microchip under the skin containing an identification number that can be scanned at a vet's office or animal shelter. The microchip registry is contacted and the company uses the ID number to look up your information from a database.

Some towns require licenses for dogs, so be sure to check with your town clerk.

For more information, speak with a vet

There are many dogs, young and old, waiting to be adopted from animal shelters and rescue groups.

Words to Know

active Always keeping busy.

fetch To go after a toy and bring it back.

groomer A person who bathes and brushes dogs.

leash A chain or strap that attaches to the dog's collar.

shed When dog hair falls out so new hair can grow.

Sheltie Another name for a Shetland sheepdog.

vaccinations Shots that dogs need to stay healthy.

veterinarian (vet) A doctor for animals.

Books

Casteel, Seth. *It's a Puppy's Life*. Washington, DC: National Geographic Children's Books, 2018.

Leaf, Christina. *Shetland Sheepdogs*. Minneapolis, MN: Bellwether Media, 2017.

Stoltman, Joan. *My First Dog*. New York, NY: Gareth Stevens Publishing, 2017.

Websites

American Canine Association Inc., Kids Corner
www.acakids.com
Visit the official website of the American Canine Association.

National Geographic for Kids, Pet Central
kids.nationalgeographic.com/explore/pet-central
Learn more about dogs and other pets at the official site of the National Geographic Society for Kids.

INDEX